HAL•LEONARD®
RECORDER
SONGBOOK

STAR WARS®

STAR WARS

MUSIC BY JOHN WILLIAMS

ISBN 978-1-4768-7465-4

HAL•LEONARD®

Visit Hal Leonard Online at
www.halleonard.com

Contact us:
Hal Leonard
7777 West Bluemound Road
Milwaukee, WI 53213
Email: info@halleonard.com

In Europe, contact:
Hal Leonard Europe Limited
42 Wigmore Street
Marylebone, London, W1U 2RN
Email: info@halleonardeurope.com

In Australia, contact:
Hal Leonard Australia Pty. Ltd.
4 Lentara Court
Cheltenham, Victoria, 3192 Australia
Email: info@halleonard.com.au

ACROSS THE STARS

Love Theme from STAR WARS: EPISODE II - ATTACK OF THE CLONES

RECORDER

Music by
JOHN WILLIAMS

Appassionato

mf

mp

rit. e dim.

THE ARENA
from STAR WARS

RECORDER

Music by
JOHN WILLIAMS

CANTINA BAND
from STAR WARS: EPISODE IV - A NEW HOPE

RECORDER

Music by
JOHN WILLIAMS

DUEL OF THE FATES

from STAR WARS: EPISODE I - THE PHANTOM MENACE

RECORDER

Music by
JOHN WILLIAMS

HAN SOLO AND THE PRINCESS

RECORDER

Music by
JOHN WILLIAMS

THE IMPERIAL MARCH
(Darth Vader's Theme)
from THE EMPIRE STRIKES BACK - A Twentieth Century-Fox Release

RECORDER

Music by
JOHN WILLIAMS

LUKE AND LEIA

from STAR WARS: EPISODE VI - RETURN OF THE JEDI

RECORDER

Music by
JOHN WILLIAMS

MAY THE FORCE BE WITH YOU

RECORDER

Music by
JOHN WILLIAMS

PARADE OF THE EWOKS

from STAR WARS: EPISODE VI - RETURN OF THE JEDI

RECORDER

Music by
JOHN WILLIAMS

PRINCESS LEIA'S THEME

from STAR WARS - A Twentieth Century-Fox Release

RECORDER

Music by
JOHN WILLIAMS

QUI-GON'S FUNERAL

from STAR WARS: EPISODE I - THE PHANTOM MENACE

RECORDER

Music by
JOHN WILLIAMS

Solemnly

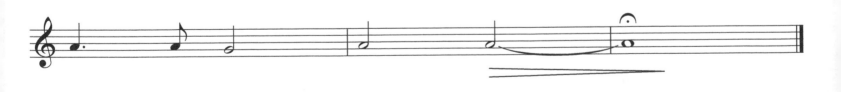

STAR WARS
(Main Theme)

from STAR WARS, THE EMPIRE STRIKES BACK and RETURN OF THE JEDI - Twentieth Century-Fox Releases

RECORDER

Music by
JOHN WILLIAMS

THE THRONE ROOM (AND END TITLE)

from STAR WARS: EPISODE IV - A NEW HOPE

RECORDER

Music by
JOHN WILLIAMS

VICTORY CELEBRATION

RECORDER

Music by
JOHN WILLIAMS

Moderate Samba

YODA'S THEME

from THE EMPIRE STRIKES BACK - A Twentieth Century-Fox Release

RECORDER

Music by
JOHN WILLIAMS

FINGERING CHART

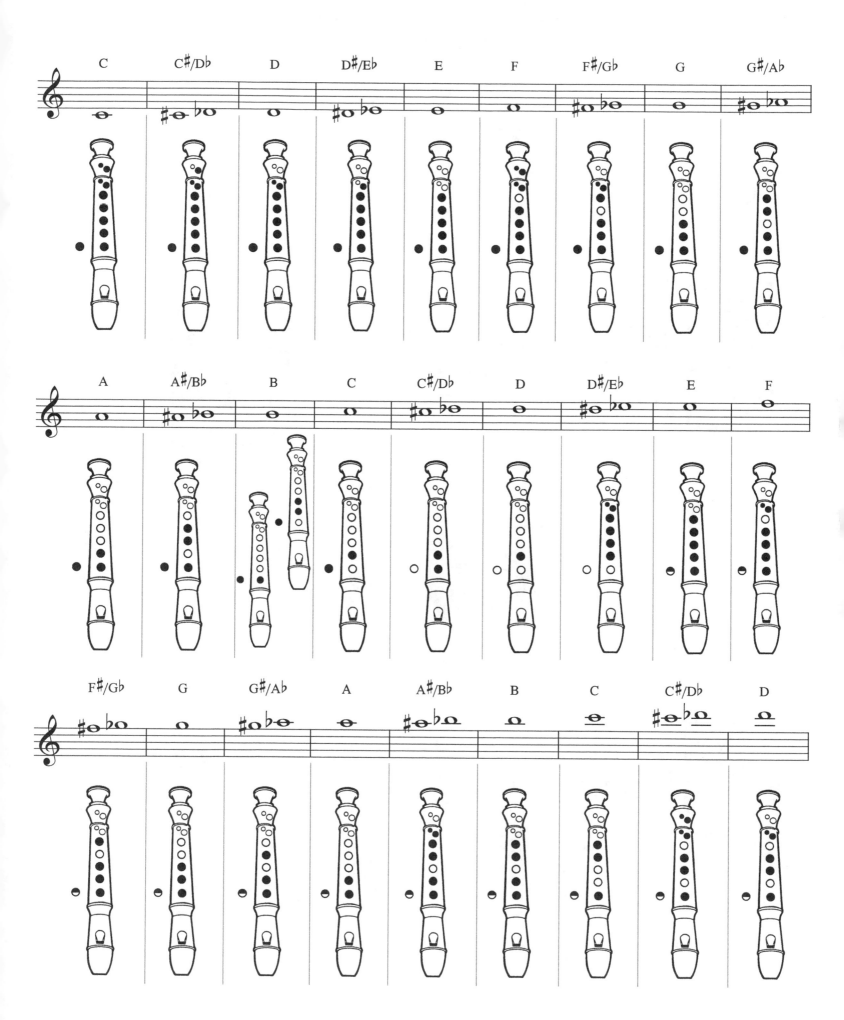

Your Favorite Songs Arranged for Recorder

RECORDER SONGBOOK

THE BEATLES

Recorder arrangements for 18 Fab Four hits, including: All My Loving • Come Together • Day Tripper • Eight Days a Week • Hey Jude • In My Life • Let It Be • Michelle • Norwegian Wood • Penny Lane • With a Little Help from My Friends • Yesterday • and more. Includes a fingering chart.

00710152 .... $7.99

BROADWAY FAVORITES

13 favorite showtunes arranged for recorder: Any Dream Will Do • As Long as He Needs Me • Consider Yourself • Getting to Know You • I Dreamed a Dream • Make Someone Happy • Memory • On a Clear Day (You Can See Forever) • On My Own • People • Sunrise, Sunset • Tomorrow • We Built This City.

00710141 .... $7.99

CLASSICAL FAVORITES

Now recorder players can play 15 of their favorite classical music selections, in arrangements for recorder solo. Titles include: Habañera (from Bizet's *Carmen*) • Lullaby (Cradle Song) (Brahms) • Ode to Joy (from Beethoven's *Symphony, No. 9*) • Panis Angelicus (O Lord Most Holy) (Franck) • Theme from Swan Lake (Tchaikovsky) • Symphony No. 9 in E Minor (from Dvorak's *From the New World*) • and more.

00710055 .... $6.99

DISNEY HITS

15 beloved Disney hits arranged for the recorder, complete with a fingering chart! Songs: The Bare Necessities • Colors of the Wind • A Dream Is a Wish Your Heart Makes • Part of Your World • Reflection • Someday • A Spoonful of Sugar • When She Loved Me • Whistle While You Work • You'll Be in My Heart • You've Got a Friend in Me • Zip-A-Dee-Doo-Dah • and more!

00710052 .... $7.99

DISNEY MOVIE FAVORITES

Nine Disney classics arranged for recorder solo or duet: Be Our Guest • Beauty and the Beast • Can You Feel the Love Tonight • Circle of Life • Friend like Me • I Just Can't Wait to Be King • Kiss the Girl • Under the Sea • A Whole New World. Includes a helpful fingering chart.

00710409 .... $7.99

WALT DISNEY FAVORITES

Newly revised, this collection features 13 Disney hits arranged for recorder solo or duet, plus a handy fingering chart! Songs: The Aristocats • Candle on the Water • Chim Chim Cher-ee • Heigh-Ho • It's a Small World • Mickey Mouse March • Once upon a Dream • The Siamese Cat Song • Some Day My Prince Will Come • Supercalifragilisticexpialidocious • When You Wish upon a Star • Who's Afraid of the Big Bad Wolf? • Winnie the Pooh.

00710100 .... $7.99

FAVORITE MOVIE THEMES – 2ND EDITION

14 film favorites for recorder: Chariots of Fire • Dancing Queen • Forrest Gump – Main Title • He's a Pirate • I'm a Believer • It Will Rain • Mission: Impossible Theme • My Heart Will Go On • Tears in Heaven • and more.

00841306 .... $7.99

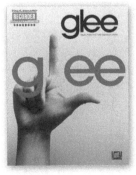

GLEE

Blow your heart out with this collection of 13 *Glee* standouts, arranged for the recorder – complete with a helpful fingering chart! Contains: Alone • Bad Romance • Defying Gravity • Don't Stop Believin' • Dream On • Hello • Lean on Me • Like a Prayer • No Air • Proud Mary • Rehab • The Safety Dance • Sweet Caroline.

00710056 .... $7.99

KIDS' SONGS

Features 13 songs kids adore, arranged for the recorder: The Addams Family Theme • Alley Cat Song • The Candy Man • Everything Is Beautiful • The Hokey Pokey • I Whistle a Happy Tune • Peter Cottontail • Puff the Magic Dragon • Sesame Street Theme • Sing • Take Me Out to the Ball Game • This Land Is Your Land • Won't You Be My Neighbor?. Includes a helpful fingering chart.

00710051 .... $7.99

STAR WARS

Features 15 iconic themes from all the *Star Wars* movies arranged for recorder! Includes: The Arena • Cantina Band • The Imperial March (Darth Vader's Theme) • May the Force Be with You • Parade of the Ewoks • Princess Leia's Theme • Star Wars (Main Theme) • Victory Celebration • Yoda's Theme • and more. Students will love playing these familiar themes while advancing through their recorder lessons!

00110292 .... $7.99

TAYLOR SWIFT

15 Swift hits arranged for recorder, including: Back to December • Eyes Open • Love Story • Mean • Should've Said No • Speak Now • Teardrops on My Guitar • Today Was a Fairytale • White Horse • You Belong with Me • and more!

00110275 .... $8.99

HAL•LEONARD®

7777 W. BLUEMOUND RD. P.O. BOX 13819
MILWAUKEE, WISCONSIN 53213

www.halleonard.com

Prices, contents, and availability subject to change without notice.
Disney Characters and Artwork TM & © 2018 Disney

0422
026